For every woman looking to reach their dreams by breaking free
from the stronghold of perfectionism!

Dedication
This book is dedicated to my two daughters Kaelyn and Kamryn.
Thank you for showing me that even in my imperfection you still
love me the same.

Welcome to *Progress Over Perfection*. This book was created to help support women who are struggling with perfectionism. This is a "no judgement zone". All that is shared comes from a place of understanding, and most importantly, it is said in love.

Let me show you how to break free…

Table of Contents

Acknowledgments

The first acknowledgement goes to my Father, Jesus Christ. This book would not be possible without you. I honor you and praise you for all that you have done in my life and all that you continue to do. Every dream I set, you supersede what I imagine. I love you!

To my daughter, Kaelyn: I am so proud of you. As an author, you know the work that it takes and have continued to support my dreams. Your drive motivates me more than you can imagine. Princess, you have a heart of gold, and I pray that you never change that. I love you and I thank God that I am blessed to be your mama.

To my daughter Kamryn: I am so honored to be your mother. Before you were born I rarely lived life outside of my comfort zone. Each day you confirm why I have to embrace the new and uncertain territories. Your creativity is one of a kind and it truly inspires me. I love you so much and thank God each and every moment I get with you.

Foreword

By: Erica Anderson Thomas

Writer and Entrepreneur

Founder of Kingdom Helper and Inner Beauty Reigns

Perfection has become a standard by which we gauge different areas of our lives. It has caused many to fail as a result of attempting to meet a mark that was actually unattainable, by means of setting unrealistic expectations. The image of perfection often misleads us to believe half-truths and even "untruths" about the lives of others. Most of all, I have found that the idea of perfection has held us hostage to those unrealistic expectations to the point of paralyzing us. Ask yourself, "What can I accomplish if I feel paralyzed?" We know the answer to this question. You accomplish NOTHING.

The fallacy of perfection sometimes prevents us from moving forward, because we feel hindered by the process when things don't turn out the way we want them to. We can think of a myriad of situations in which this could apply. We often allow our expectations as well as the perception of perfection to jade us to reality and to this simple fact: LIFE HAPPENS.

If the event is not picture perfect, it's ok! If the business deal fell through, there will be other opportunities! If the relationship didn't unfold in the way you anticipated, life goes on! There is freedom in not forcing yourself to be a perfectionist.

I have had the honor and great pleasure of editing other publications written by Nicolya including *Making Your Message Your Masterpiece* and *The Goal Getter Guide.* It never ceases to amaze me how sincere and relatable Nicolya is as she writes. Furthermore, I have a great appreciation for the transparency of each of her books. It takes great courage to peel back those layers and share with such transparency, but I also know that you will receive information that will help you understand the reason why it is important to take the steps necessary to improve the quality of your life.

With experience comes wisdom for those who are open to receive it. Nicolya's writing style comes with a lot of golden nuggets and makes each of her books worth reading. As you take in the wisdom shared in the following pages, prepare your heart and mind to experience a full realm of transformation in your life. Prepare yourself to release, receive and reflect as you go through this process. I have no doubt that the application of the principles and strategies shared in *Progress Over Perfection* will lead to you having a progressive and more productive life.

Intro

"Striving for excellence motivates you. Striving for perfection is demoralizing."
-Harriet Braiker

Hi, I am Nicolya and I am a recovering perfectionist. I have been clean for almost one year, although I often have many slip-ups. You get the picture. All jokes aside, I truly am overcoming my ways as a perfectionist. For years, I battled with this idea that I had to be perfect. To be honest, I tried to make this book perfect, all while I was writing about how that was impossible. I was consumed with the thought that everything I put effort into had to come out the best way possible. I did this when I cleaned the house, I did this at my job, with my business and I even did it in my parenting. Needless to say I got burned out. I was putting in crazy hours trying to make everything perfect. Regardless of what I did, nothing ever felt good enough. My house was never clean enough, even though I got tons of compliments. My business was not standing out enough, although I got clients. My work projects were too overwhelming, even though I could finish them in less time than my coworkers. My ability to parent my daughters never felt like it met my expectations. But, that was my problem. The expectations that I had for myself were ridiculous. I had this motto that if it was not going to be perfect there was no point in doing it.

In one aspect, I believe that this mentality showed that I cared about the task at hand. However, I also put a ton of unnecessary pressure on myself. I would start a project, get half way through and scrap it. I would turn down opportunities because I didn't feel "perfect" enough to do them. Needless to say, my perfectionism was keeping me stuck. I knew that it was a problem. I just did not know how to break free. I'd like to say that I had this huge "a-ha moment" that broke me free, but it was not like that. As a woman who is in love with personal development, I am ALWAYS looking for ways to develop more into who I desire to be. One day, I randomly sat down to process through my perfectionism. I was working on writing my first book. This was a desire of mine for years but I would often lose motivation when my writing did not come off as good enough. It got so bad that I would even forget the topic that I wanted to write about because I did not jump on the idea quick enough. After months of writing and tossing my writing away because it was not good enough, I decided I would keep writing. After my writing session a question popped into my head: "What has being perfect cost you?" It was such a random question because I was asking myself this. I think I knew deep down that my perfectionism was taking a toll on my life. I did not really want to answer the question, but I knew I had to. So I listed all of the things that I lost due to my perfectionism. At that time I had lost book ideas, speaking engagements, clients and family opportunities. The list could go on. When I realized how much money I lost, I got frustrated. The anger that I felt did something for me. It caused me to decide to create a strategy that I could use to get out of my rut. And that is just what I did.

On September 25, 2017 I had a dream that I was talking to women all around the world about how to break free of their perfectionistic hold. I woke up the next morning and wrote 28 pages without stopping. Later that day I had a client of mine reach out about struggling with perfectionism and how it was preventing her from doing anything worthwhile. She mentioned how she was always playing safe in order to ensure the "perfect" outcome. I knew it was a sign that I had to write my book. I wanted to help women just like her to understand that progress is what matters, not perfection. I wanted women to know the damaging effects of believing that they have to be perfect. That is why this book was written. It is a simple strategy to follow for you struggling perfectionists to create success on reasonable terms. You see, as perfectionists we aim for success, but the target is way out of bounds. In this book I will talk with you about the trouble that perfectionism causes and the best system to break out of the hold it has on your life. I am doing this because breaking free was one of the best choices I have ever made. If I had held onto my perfectionism I would have never written any of my books, started my business, written my blogs or for magazines. I would have never broken free from my comfort zone. I would have never grown.

Now you did not pick this book up because you were bored. You either received this book or bought it because you know something needs to change. So congratulations to you for taking the first step which is recognizing that you struggle with perfectionism. You are in great company and you will walk away with a great strategy to start living life without all of the preconceived notions of perfection.

Progress Over Perfection means that you do not have to struggle to be perfect, you just have to make progress toward your goals a little at a time. I read a very impactful book about two years ago called *The Slight Edge*. The premise of this book is that every step we take either pushes us toward our goals or further away from them. This is exactly what I want you to take away from this book.

Reflection

Are you proud of your achievements or are you self-critical, judgmental and lacking in compassion towards yourself?

Do you feel you must work harder, longer and better than others?

Do you fear failure?

Do you link self-worth to your achievements rather than the qualities you offer as a person?

What is Perfectionism?

"I am a perfectionist…..to the point of insanity."
-Tom Ford

So what exactly is perfectionism? I had heard of it, but for some reason I assumed that it only applied to people who wanted to be perfect in every aspect of their life. I had no clue that even striving for perfection in one area is still perfectionism. You see I did not strive for perfectionism in every role in my life. It was in very specific roles and therefore I thought I was clear from the title of being a perfectionist. According to Wikipedia, perfectionism is a personality trait characterized by a person's striving for flawlessness and setting high performance standards, accompanied by critical self-evaluations and concerns regarding others' evaluations. I define perfectionism as this idea that you can have no flaws and all of the work you do has to reflect this. Perfectionists have a tendency to set standards that are so high that they either cannot be met, or are only met with a great amount of difficulty.

Perfectionism has a major impact on the people who aim for it. It affects how one thinks, behaves, and feels. Perfectionism can make you feel depressed, frustrated, anxious, and even angry. The voice of perfectionism says that your efforts are not good enough and that you should always have everything under control. This leads to feelings of overwhelm and in turn causes you to feel burned out. The person who battles with perfectionism is never convinced of their self-worth and battles with goals or ideas to the point of exhaustion. This happens because you constantly criticize yourself for not doing a good enough job after spending a lot of time and effort on a task. I am now able to see how perfectionism manifested in my life and the impact that it had on me. This is what inspired me to write this book.

It has been said that approximately 30% of the general population suffer from some form of perfectionism. Personally, I wonder if the number is higher, but some don't recognize it or do not want to admit it. Oftentimes when people live with perfectionism for a long period of time, they write it off as normal behavior. People make excuses, such as saying they want to do well and that is just the way it shows up. Often people use perfectionistic tendencies as an excuse for being dedicated to their goals. It is wonderful to love your goals and work hard for them, but it becomes dangerous when you are going crazy trying to make them happen perfectly.
It is also noted that most of those who struggle with perfectionism are gifted in one area or another. Perfectionists value and foster

excellence and strive to meet important goals. In certain areas, like sports and science, perfectionism is not just tolerated but encouraged. The problem is that perfectionism is not possible and so when we strive for things that are not possible we will always feel let down.

Perfectionists are extremely vulnerable to distress, often haunted by a chronic sense of failure. Indecisiveness is a close companion to procrastination, as well as shame. Perfectionism is said to have developed as a result of having **feelings of inferiority** or of being less than others. When a child experiences these feelings he develops an affinity for perfectionism in order to maintain a sense of superiority over his friends and over his environment. Another negative result of the development of perfectionism is that the child hides his defects from others. After all, if he did everything perfectly then no one would be able to see the hidden defects.

Many perfectionists grew up in a home with parents or guardians who either directly or indirectly communicated that they were not good enough. These were often confusing messages for the children. The messages included both praise and criticism simultaneously. For example:

- "That was nice, but I bet you could do better."
- "Yeah, you remembered to wash the floor, but not how I like it. You missed several spots'.
- "Yeah, a "B" is great, but your sister got an "A".
- "Good job on your concert, next time I come make sure you sing louder so I can hear you."

Parents do not always intend to come off that way, but these types of statements can impact children in ways they are not even aware of. It sends the message to the children that their best is not good enough. They begin to feel inadequate and therefore they grow into adults who feel the need to prove themselves through being perfect. As you can tell it is a cycle.

Reflection

What are your feelings about perfectionism?

Do you feel vulnerable to distress?

What was your household like growing up?

What other things contribute to your perfectionism?

Am I a Perfectionist?

"Perfectionism doesn't make you feel perfect, it makes you feel inadequate."
-Maria Shriver

I hate to break it to you, but if you grabbed this book, or someone referred it to you, there is a good chance that you are indeed a perfectionist. I am not judging though, because I too am one….well, was one. I say that because if you have perfectionistic tendencies they are always there, you just learn to cope with them in more different ways. Now being a perfectionist is not like you have to walk around with a scarlet letter "P" on your head and it is not something you have to be ashamed of. There are some great things about being a perfectionist. One thing that comes to mind is your passion for your work. If you care enough to make it perfect that means you really care about what you're working on. Take me for example. When I got pregnant, I read every single parenting book you could imagine. I attended classes and joined different groups. I was all set up to be the perfect parent. I had one daughter, then I had another. What I learned is that it does not matter how many books you read, how much practice you have or how many people you talk to. We are human we are bound to fail. At first I took that personal, but I reframed that thinking and told myself, the reason I wanted to be perfect is because I believe my kids deserve the best. To this day, I still want to be the perfect mommy, but I have learned that to be perfect is to show my daughters that I am human. That I fall short and that it is okay because I still did my absolute best.

I am going to be vulnerable for a minute. I am an overachiever and an extreme perfectionist to the point that it caused me so much pain. As a perfectionist there were some major things happening that made me realize that my perfectionism had gotten out of control. One major sign was that I would not allow myself to dream BIG for fear of the idea that the goal I went for would not be perfect or would not be reached. I boxed myself in. For years I played so small and was not ever working toward my potential. Then I started to be consumed with guilt of not accomplishing all that I wanted to. That guilt and desire to be perfect took over my life. I stopped taking risks for fear of making mistakes again. It was a cycle that prevented me from reaching my goals and kept me always feeling unqualified/ not good enough.

There are several key things that you can do that can help you to confirm whether your perfectionism is out of control. One is having a habit of only trying things that you know you can do perfectly. Another is having the mentality of "go hard or go home". Basically this means that you are only going to put your best foot forward or no foot at all. Another key indicator of being a perfectionist is crying over spilled milk. This happens when you make a big deal over things that did not turn out well, even though it can't be changed and it is over with.

Perfectionists often have a hard time being vulnerable with others due to fear of being judged or misunderstood. The silly thing is that they are often critical of others. No matter what you accomplish you are never "there" yet.

Typically, perfectionists are neat in their appearance and are well organized. They are known as tidy and clean. They are driven, disciplined and motivated. They seem to push themselves harder than most other people do. On the outside, perfectionists usually appear to be very competent and confident individuals. They are often looked up to or envied by other people because they seem to "have it all together." They also seem to make it "look easy".

The trouble is that is how they appear to be. On the inside they do not feel perfect, nor do they feel like they always have control over their own lives. Perfectionists often have trouble making decisions. They become consumed about the idea that they may make the wrong choice that they fail to reach any conclusion. Sometimes they allow other people to make decisions for them, therefore allowing the other people to assume responsibility for the outcome. I have ALWAYS battled with decision making for this exact reason. I could not handle the pressure of making decisions. When I did and things went wrong, the feelings were unbearable. I used to enjoy when things were easy and the decisions were already made because I had less things I had to be "perfect" at doing.

Perfectionists are often indecisive and are sometimes apprehensive about taking risks, especially if their personal reputation is on the line. This is very overwhelming because the desire to perfect with so many things at once is daunting. Taking risks requires the perfectionist to step into the unknown and this can be quite uncomfortable.

Each person has a set of beliefs about themselves, other people, and the world and about the future. These beliefs are used to interpret the experiences in our life, and they strongly influence our emotional reactions. Here are some common phrases that perfectionists say:

- I should always be on top of things.
- I must do this right.
- It has to be done perfectly or not at all.
- I have to_____.
- This is not good enough.

Now take a minute to ask yourself:

- Do you ever have trouble meeting your own standards?
- Do you often feel easily frustrated when trying to meet other's standards?
- Have people told you previously that your standards are too high?

Perfectionism is about avoiding feelings of shame, judgment and inadequacy. ***By being perfect, you have permission to not feel bad about yourself.*** However, you never feel good enough about yourself. Perfectionists aren't usually trying to achieve something great. They're trying to avoid something negative.

A perfectionist can enjoy a few perks. Many people admire perfectionists. However, the disadvantages usually aren't worth it. Here are some common misconceptions of perfectionists:

- Black-and-white thinking (e.g., "Anything less than perfection is a failure")
- Catastrophic thinking (e.g., "If I make a mistake in front of my coworkers, I won't be able to survive the embarrassment")
- Probability overestimation (e.g., "Although I spent all night preparing for a presentation, I know I won't do well")
- "Should" statements (e.g., "I should never make mistakes" or "I should always be able to predict problems before they occur.")

Being a perfectionist has several disadvantages:

1.   **You waste a lot of time.** Some things don't require a high level of attention, but for a perfectionist to get it done "right" it will

take a great deal of both time and attention. To spend more time than necessary is a waste of an important resource: your time.

2.	**It creates a lot of stress.** When there's only one way to be successful at something, there's no room for error. This type of black and white thinking will cause feelings of overwhelm, sadness and frustration. Perfectionists have a constant anxiety that can't be completely contained.

3.	**You lose sight of the big picture.** Bogging yourself down with insignificant details can limit your awareness of the bigger objective.

4.	**You're never happy with your results.** You might be satisfied, but you're never happy. This is because nothing can ever be 100% perfect so the failure to reach that level of perfectionism causes some major unhappiness and sometimes even depression.

Signs to be aware of when perfectionism gets out of hand:

1.	**You're judgmental of others.** Your standards of acceptability are so high that no one, not yourself, not your loved ones, can consistently achieve them. You may find your friends or family feeling like they cannot meet your expectations.

2.	**You're too hard on yourself.** You can't live up to your expectations either. This leads to feelings of disappointment, guilt and even shame. Are you more successful than most of the people you know, but less pleased with yourself than they are with themselves? This answer will speak volumes. Ask yourself, do you find it hard to be proud of yourself?

3.	**You procrastinate excessively.** The need to be perfect creates anxiety and makes it hard to get started. It feels like getting started is the hardest part and that you won't be able to make it happen.

Rate these statements for yourself to see if you are struggling with perfectionism:

1- Never
2- Sometimes
3-Always

_____ I must be perfect or I will be rejected.

_____ If I make a mistake, the outcome will be horrible.

_____ If I do it perfectly, then I will be accepted by myself and by others.

_____ I must be perfect or I will be embarrassed, judged or laughed at.

_____ When I achieve perfection, I will find inner peace.

_____ If I make a mistake, then I feel worthless.

_____ I'm not good enough. I must keep trying until it is perfect.

_____ No matter what I do I feel like I will never be good enough.

_____ Things have to be done perfectly or not at all.

_____ My feelings are based on me accomplishing my goals perfectly.

If you received mostly threes, you struggle with perfectionism. Don't worry. Keep reading, and you will learn how to work through your perfectionism and reach reasonable goals.

If you received mostly twos you are on the brink of perfectionism and definitely have some perfectionist tendencies. This book will give you some great strategies to keep you from tipping the scale and falling into the perfectionism trap.

If you received mostly ones you are doing well and do not often struggle with perfectionism. The outlook you have on your accomplishments is reasonable.

Reflection

What drives your perfectionism?

Do you just enjoy having a high standard or does perfectionism help keep your self-esteem high and make you feel worthy?

In what ways are you a perfectionist?

Is it mainly work/performance based, is it related to personal grooming or health, the home, or another area of your life?

Stress and Perfectionism

"When perfectionism is driving, shame is always riding shotgun."
-Brene Brown

Did you know that aiming for perfection actually increases your stress level? Many people believe that striving for perfection actually increases the likelihood that you will be successful. Have you ever heard the quote, "Reach for the sky because if you fail, at least you will fall amongst the stars."? The reality is that aiming for perfection does not increase perfection it actually causes you more stress. Sometimes it even increases failure, because you are not trying at all.

Ultimately, the thoughts of a perfectionist are self-sabotaging, and actually in turn have a negative impact on the results and achievements because we don't live in a perfect world. Those of us who have developed perfectionism continue to face letdowns, and disappointments that ruin our emotions, mood and life. Perfectionism truly becomes a problem when it causes emotional wear and tear on your body. It also is a problem when it keeps you from succeeding or from being truly happy.

There is a cost to setting unrealistic goals and expecting to be perfect. When you desire to be perfect you will always feel frustrated and disappointed when you fail. On the other hand when you do succeed, you still may not feel good about it because you think you "should" have done better. Imagine the weight of all of that disappointment if you continue to set goals this way for the rest of your life. This disappointment will become overwhelming and will increase your stress. It can also cause you to avoid setting goals for fear of not reaching them perfectly. This step will keep you stuck in your life, and you won't reach much of anything because at that point you're not even striving for anything.

There is a double edge sword to perfection. Perfectionism is driven by both a desire to do well and a fear of the consequences of not doing well. This causes the reach for perfection to be painful. It is a great thing to give your best effort, to go the extra mile, and to take pride in one's performance. However, when you feel as though you keep falling short, that you never seem to get things just right, you become self-conscious and you feel criticized by others. These are not good feelings. The emotional stress that can be caused by trying to reach perfection along with the failure to achieve this impossible goal can evolve into even more stress.

The emotional consequences of perfectionism include fear of making mistakes, stress from the pressure to perform, and self-consciousness from feeling both self-confidence and self-doubt. Trying to be perfect often misconstrues your thinking. It tricks you to believe that what you do will never be good enough. In turn, you fear that you will be judged, misunderstood, or inadequate. All in all perfectionism can definitely increase fear. Here are five signs that show if you have been consumed in fear.

1. Failing makes you worry about what other people think about you.
2. Failing makes you worry about your ability to pursue the future you desire.
3. Failing makes you worry about how smart or capable you are.
4. Failing makes you worry about disappointing people whose opinion you value.
5. You tend to tell people beforehand that you don't expect to succeed in order to lower their expectations.

Fear is the number one factor that can prevent us from setting BIG goals and going after them. Fear is our body's response to potential danger. It can have a negative impact on our life. Have you ever heard of fight or freeze? Freeze means you stop what you are doing and focus on the fearful stimulus to decide what to do next. This is what I call being stuck. Fear can put us in situations where we feel hopeless to move. People who stay here often obsess about their situation, they complain, but they never move or take action. This is where a perfectionist stops. They live in fear of not being perfect and therefore do not take the next steps. When you respond with fear, it leads to the feeling stuck, feelings of hopelessness and could potentially lead to depression.

Many people are unaware that perfectionists are more vulnerable to depression when stressful events occur. These events leave them feeling as though they are not good enough. The attitudes and beliefs can set a person up to be disappointed, given that achieving perfection on a consistent basis is impossible. What's more, perfectionists who have grown up around the idea that they have to be perfect could be extremely sensitive to events that highlight their "failures". Here are signs that your perfectionism tendencies are causing you more stress:

1. It is impossible for you to keep a realistic perspective
2. You are consumed with the idea that perfection exists and you keep looking for it.
3. You are not willing to be flexible with your approach.
4. You are only focused on your results.
5. You are often procrastinating.

If you are aware that you have been feeling more stress lately, maybe it is time to assess whether you are being a perfectionist. Maybe you're trying to be the perfect spouse, the perfect parent, or a perfect employee. You have to let go of the idea of being perfect. No matter what you do or how hard you try, things will never be perfect. Don't strive for perfection. Strive to do your best. When you change your mentality, you will reduce the amount of stress you have been putting on yourself. More importantly you will feel a lot better!

Reflection

Do you recognize that the most successful people know how to "play"? Do you balance work and play?

What stressors have been added to your life as a result of you dealing with perfectionism?

Do you think in shades of grey or in extremes?

Do you see positives in your performance or do you only focus on the negatives?

Do you often discount your own achievements?

Procrastination and Perfectionism

"Don't let your want for perfection become procrastination."
-Danielle LaPorte

How often do you set out to work on something, only to avoid it later? How many times are you reminded that you have a task to complete, but you're more interested in scrolling through social media to kill time? I have been there. In fact, yesterday while writing this book I had to use some crafty strategies to make sure I put my phone down and chose to write instead. Procrastination is the action of delaying or postponing something. Often you procrastinate because of a fear of failure, hard tasks, confusion or discomfort. What would happen if you could let go of wanting things to be easy, successful and comfortable? What would happen if you just accept that there is a wide range of experiences, and embrace that truth?

It has been said that 20% of people procrastinate. This is not an accident or by chance. Procrastination is a learned habit, which can be challenging to overcome. It prevents your success which is never beneficial and this is why I want to help you curb the desire to participate in it. Procrastination allows us to avoid what we are supposed to do and focus on things that are easier and safer.

Everyone knows that procrastination is bad, right? Everyone assumes that perfectionism is fine. That is so wrong. The two tend to appear together, forming an infinite loop that can destroy your productivity and even your outlook. Out of the two terms, perfectionism seems to be more subtle and more difficult to identify. As far as procrastination, it is often followed by immediate consequences. This unreasonable striving for perfection stems from attempts to preserve a sense of self-worth that hinges on the expectations of others. It is often referred to as "the highest form of self-abuse" because perfection simply doesn't exist. More importantly, perfection is rarely needed in day-to-day working and living situations.

Procrastination is often a symptom of perfectionism. Perfectionists fear being unable to complete a task perfectly, therefore they put it off as long as possible. This stems from the fear that not meeting the goal means that there is something bad, something wrong or something unworthy inside of them. Furthermore, perfectionists fear that failure will invoke criticism or ridicule from both internal and external. The higher the fear of failure and ridicule, the more perfectionists procrastinate. Most people believe that procrastination is actually a form of laziness. In reality, procrastination is not laziness. It's more of a misguided sense of activity based on a low tolerance for frustration and failure.

Here is an example: You have a deadline quickly approaching. However, instead of doing the work to meet the goal, you are fiddling with miscellaneous things like checking email, social media, watching videos, talking on the phone, surfing blogs and forums. You know you should be working, but you just don't feel like doing anything. Needless to say you miss the deadline, and now you feel guilty. Why can't I just focus? Why can't I get what I need to get done? Why am I so easily distracted? You beat yourself up with loads of questions.

The truth is distractions serve us. Distractions are comfortable and that is often why we fall back on them. It feels familiar and to some extent it feels safe. It is much like our comfort zone. Or comfort zone feels familiar, safe and comfortable therefore when we come up with ideas or other people do to break free it feels impossible or completely out of the norm.

Despite the negative repercussions of perfectionism and procrastination, it is a cycle people return to simply because it is what they know. But it is critical to break the loop. For one, you waste valuable time beating yourself up mentally by putting off tasks that you signed yourself up to do. And by "valuable time," I mean that the time does not come back. We can't rewind or recycle time...it is a HOT COMMODITY. Therefore, think of what you are doing with the time you have that is extremely valuable. Are you scrolling or are you working? After all, do you **really** want to look at all your friends' Facebook pics instead of writing the book you have dreamed of for ten years?

Both perfectionism and procrastination have long term impacts on your mental and physical health. The dysfunctional thinking of perfectionism can be toxic. This can often lead to discouragement, self-doubt and mental exhaustion. Procrastination is equally damaging. Not only do procrastinators squander their precious resources of time, attention and focus, but the constant stress caused by procrastination eventually leads to problems like compromised immunity, digestive problems and insomnia. Remember, time is one of our most valuable assets so wasting it will never feel good. And wasting it will never bring about the rewards that you are seeking.

When your fears are based on whether your outcome will be "good enough", here are some tips to entice your brain into thinking differently:

- Don't wait for the conditions to be perfect to get started. Trust and believe that you have everything that you need to get going on the task, and that you will discover any additional resources that you need along the way. This will happen, trust me I have experienced it.
- Accept that what you are doing will never be perfect. Keep in mind that you have to start *somewhere and the more you practice, the better it will be*. For example, my first book is by far my worst book. With practice, I have gotten better at writing. It was the biggest lesson in my life that helped me to understand that I can reach goals without having to be perfect. Many ridiculously successful ideas have had humble beginnings. Your idea is no different. You can always change your creation later, but get it out the door — don't wait until it's flawless. By then, it may be too late.
- Be aware of unrealistic expectations that you have set for yourself. Free yourself from the "black and white" thinking. Go over the *Best/Worst/Real* exercise: whatever tasks you feel compelled to do perfectly (and thus are procrastinating on), write down what you believe could be the Best Case Scenario, the Worst Case Scenario, and what is most likely to be the Realistic Scenario. The Realistic Scenario will be neutral. This will highlight how unrealistic your fears often are. This activity always helps me to step out on my fears and work on the task anyways.

- <u>Remember that no one else cares and no one else really matters.</u> Most people are so wrapped up with themselves that they won't notice any "slip" on your part. We are ALWAYS our own worst critic. Let go of your desire to impress others and embrace being human. After all, that is what you are.
- <u>Understand the difference between excellence and perfection.</u> Excellence stems from enjoying and learning from an experience, which allows you to develop confidence. Perfection on the other hand fosters negative feelings from any perceived mistakes made, regardless of the excellence of performance.
- <u>Remember the real reason you started.</u> When I wrote my first book I wanted to impact women around the world. My book did not have to be perfect to do that. As a matter of fact, being imperfect was what truly had the biggest impact on my readers. Once I remembered the purpose behind my project I was able to keep pushing through those negative thoughts I consumed myself with. Take some time to really identify why you want to do this and keep this on your mind throughout the project.

Reflection

Do you get things done or are you holding back because you don't feel good enough?

Are you damaging your productivity and heightening your anxiety because of your habit of procrastinating?

How has procrastination impacted you?

Why do you think it is important to change your tendency to procrastinate?

Guilt and Perfectionism

"When things are perfect that is when you need to worry the most." -Drew Barrymore

Guilt and perfectionism are the worst combination. Underneath it all, perfectionists are often plagued by guilt and shame which is overwhelming. As a culture, we value people that are perfectionists and make it seem like this is the ideal way to be. As you know if you are a perfectionist, you have the feeling that you must be flawless, and that you must please everybody. You have this idea that you must be achieving more and that you are never quite there. Most perfectionists have this belief that they always have to do more, and that they are not allowed to relax. If you're a perfectionist, your favorite phrase is, "I should ... I must ... I ought to ... I have to ..." You're always doing more, but nothing is ever good enough. If you are an average person you may have 3-5 things to do each day on your daily to do list. Perfectionists on the other hand have thirty things and feel less than if they cannot accomplish all of these things plus more. When you become consumed in these ideas you increase your depression, guilt and shame.

Guilt is an emotional warning sign that we learn during childhood. We learn that when we make poor choices, we feel guilty and then learn to make better ones. The purpose of guilt is to let us know when we have done something wrong, to help us develop a better sense of our behavior and how it affects ourselves and others. It also prompts us to re-examine our choices so that we are not making poor choices repeatedly. Now, there is such a thing as healthy guilt and that of unhealthy guilt. Healthy guilt is an important feeling and leads to positive action, but unhealthy guilt is a waste of your energy. Understanding this is a key strategy to overcoming your perfectionism.

Healthy guilt is the feeling that occurs when you have actually done something wrong - such as harming someone. This type of guilt is an important feeling, which results from having developed a conscience. This type of guilt helps to direct you with the choices you should make in the future. Healthy guilt results in taking responsibility for our choices and being accountable for our actions. When we have not behaved in a way that is in our highest good and for the greater good of all, our loving adult self will feel remorse and take over, doing whatever we have to do to remedy the situation.

Unhealthy guilt is not something you should feel bad for. For example you truly did your best on the project your boss asked you to complete and it still was not perfect for him. You should not be overwhelmed with guilt regarding this because truthfully you did not intentionally try to do a bad job. Many of us have been trained to believe that we are responsible for the feelings of others, so when others are angry or hurt, we feel the burden of guilt. Unless you deliberately intended to harm someone, his or her feelings are not your responsibility. You are responsible for your own intent. When you intend to harm someone, then you are responsible for the results of that.

One quote that I love is by Brene Brown. She says "Healthy striving is self-focused: 'How can I improve?'" Perfectionism is "other-focused": What will they think? When we are focused on what other people will think, we will always be let down. The truth is you can't please everyone and striving for that will always leave you feeling guilty because it can't happen. I remember one time I was working after school and I was asked to help watch the students that had after school detention. While I did not mind, the time was getting late and I had promised my children that we would do something after school. I declined the offer. I was overwhelmed with guilt because I felt that I had let my principal down although I had fun with my daughters. I was plagued with guilt from not handling the situation perfectly. I was overwhelmed with the idea that my principal would not think I was dedicated or would even consider me lazy. Is there a perfect way it could have been handled? Not at all. Could I have made everyone involved happy? Not at all. I had to do what I felt was best and not be so consumed in what others would think.

In order to break free from the unhealthy guilt you are dealing with, here are a few steps to consider:

1. Identify areas where you are trying to be perfect.
2. Recognize whether the guilt of not being perfect is healthy or unhealthy.
3. Identify how you can do your best.
4. Identify what you can learn from this situation.

5. Remind yourself that perfection does not exist in anyone.

This process takes time, but working through it will allow you to take the guilt of not being perfect off of your back.

Reflection

Currently, in which things are you expecting to be perfect?

What do you feel guilty about?

Are you dealing with unhealthy or healthy guilt in your life?

Going forward, what can you do with that guilt?

Confidence and Perfectionism

"Perfectionism is self-abuse in its highest order."
-Anne Wilson Shaef

Many people don't realize it, but being a perfectionist is often related to how you feel about yourself. For example, if you have low confidence you will often try to overcompensate through your "perfect" actions. The best way to build confidence is through embracing who you are and being authentic to that. Confidence is one of those terms we hear often but have no clue how it will fit in our lives. Confidence is our ability to believe and trust in ourselves. It is also about our ability to rely on ourselves and our abilities. When we are aiming to be perfect there is no way that we can be confident in something that is unobtainable.

With all the comparing and contrasting that happens through social media, it is difficult to be okay with being true to yourself. Authenticity is so underrated. It's more than being honest with the world. It's about being honest with yourself. There are many advantages to being authentic. *Most importantly, you'll no longer feel the need to change your words and actions to impress others.* You can relax and be yourself and actually enjoy it. Before you can be authentic, it's important to know yourself. This includes your values and goals. Authenticity becomes possible when you know what's important to you and your life matches those beliefs.

Embrace authenticity and present yourself honestly:

1.   **Give up the need to appear perfect.** Nobody in this world is perfect, except Jesus. Embrace doing your best. This means put your best foot forward, but do not concern yourself with being perfect. Being excellent is good enough. When you don't need to appear perfect, you're in the position to be honest. No one can be perfect and honest at the same time. Avoid putting on a show for the rest of the world. You'll only feel bad about yourself later. Choose to *be the best at being yourself.*

2.   **Know your values and live by them.** If you know your values and live by them consistently, you're already doing well with being authentic. In order to identify your values, make a list of your values and determine the five that are most important to you. Are you living your life according to these values? Would it be obvious to others that you hold these values? Next, decide to make your decisions based upon your values. Oftentimes we choose our values

based on other's values. This will cause confusion and frustration. Be willing to share your values with others. You will be surprised at how many people can relate to your values.

3. **Notice when you're not being authentic.** It's not easy to be authentic all the time. *You might find yourself transforming based on the situation.* An interview is a good example. Are you being authentic or pretending to be someone you're not? Are you pretending to be passionate about something you could care less about? **Of course when you are on an interview you are supposed to give your best impression, you are not supposed to pretend to be someone else.** Take note of those times when your authenticity starts to wane. Ask yourself why you are making those choices. Get an understanding on why you believe that being yourself will not help this opportunity.

4. **Know your goals.** What do you want out of life? Do you know? Are you willing to let others know? By knowing your goals, you can you live your life accordingly. This does not include goals that others have made for you. These are goals you want to reach for yourself. To do this, make a list of your short-term and long-term goals. How well do they align with your values? Identify your characteristics or passions that will help support these goals.

5. **What are your defining characteristics?** Describe yourself honestly. Now ask yourself if a casual acquaintance would describe you the same way? How about someone that knows you well? How about your closest friend? How many people know you well? If there aren't many, ask yourself why. If you're living authentically, it should be easy for someone to develop an accurate opinion of you. What are your "negative" characteristics? Are you impatient, lazy or messy? Are you willing to allow others to see these characteristics or do you attempt to hide them? We all have characteristics that we are not proud of, this means we are human!

6. **Tell the truth.** *If you're being authentic, why would you need to lie?* This especially pertains to anything you say about yourself. Admit your mistakes, weaknesses, and frailties. Share your opinions honestly and freely with those around you. I have learned that being

transparent has actually made me more relatable and improved my relationships.

7. **Simplify your life.** Get rid of everything that's extraneous. What you choose to keep will be representative of your preferences and your true self. Find your true essence by stripping away the non-essentials. Start with the clothes you never wear, the things you never use, and the activities you don't enjoy. Only keep the things that mean the most to you. I read a great book called the *Japanese Art of Tidying Up*. The premise of this book is that if you have things that no longer bring you joy then you need to get rid of it.

8. **Do what you say you'll do.** This is my favorite step because people do not often find the importance of doing what they say they will. This is your character at stake and trust me, you don't want others to think of you as the person who will doesn't follow through. Keep your word and follow through on your promises. You'll feel more congruent, and others will view you as more reliable. When your words and actions match, you're demonstrating authenticity. Life becomes easier when you're living authentically. ***You'll no longer feel the exhaustion that comes with constantly changing your opinions, attitudes, and personality to please others.*** You'll no longer feel the need to protect yourself from others. Be authentic with your thoughts, words, and actions. Invest the time in yourself and learn to be free.

Reflection

1. Does your need for getting everything right interfere with having healthy relationships?

2. Do you often criticize others for not doing things right?

3. Do you avoid situations that may be fun but you may look foolish or incompetent?

4. Does the thought of having to be perfect make you feel inadequate?

People Pleasing and Perfectionism

"At its root, perfectionism isn't really about a deep love of being meticulous. It's about fear. Fear of making a mistake. Fear of disappointing others. Fear of failure. Fear of success."

-Michael Law

People-pleasing and perfectionism stem from the effort to prove your worth. Underlying fear is a component of both elements. There is the fear that you're not good enough in the eyes others. As a result of this belief, you assume that you have to keep pleasing, achieving, and perfecting in order for people to like and want you. This is like a cycle you're stuck doing, but no matter what you do it's never enough. Perfection is impossible and pleasing everyone is also impossible, therefore it's a lose-lose situation.

Let's first address the fear. For most of my life, the fear of what other people thought of me kept me trapped. It prevented me from reaching my full potential and from enjoying life to the fullest. I threw away ideas that I had and goals I wanted to reach, all in the name of fear. But I've come to realize that everyone—those who appear confident or shy; extroverts or introverts— are struggling with our own fears. I hate to say, but glad to highlight it: you are not alone in this. When the fear of what other people think is holding you back, take a look around and remember, everyone is living with his or her own fear.

Below are the signs that highlight if you live in fear of what other people think:

1. You won't make a decision without approval from someone else.
2. You do things you don't want to do and you resent it.
3. You no longer (or never did) really know what you want.
4. You're afraid to say what you really believe.
5. You struggle to make your own decisions.
6. You are overwhelmed with thinking about what others are thinking.

To break free of this fear you have to be intentional.

1. You have to believe that you and what you want matters. To do this take some time for yourself to relearn who you really are. Take the time to remember that your expectations of pleasing everyone will never happen.
2. Ask yourself: What if other people do think badly of you? The truth is that if everyone likes you, you're probably not being true to yourself. Ask yourself "What's the worst that could happen with them not liking the real me?" Come to terms with it. It will not be the end of the world, in fact it may be a new beginning for you.
3. Decide what's truly important to you: Is what people think of you high on that list? Make a short list, post it on your fridge, send yourself reminders on your phone, and don't let critical people around you come between you and fulfillment of the things on that list.
4. Change your circle. If you have a judgmental group around you, it is imperative to change those who are speaking to you. If the people are being condescending to you then those are not the people who need to be around you at all. You want to surround yourself with people who encourage you and believe in you, not those who will cause insecurities and doubts to flare up.

By taking deliberate and purposeful steps to overcome the fear of what others think of you, you slowly regain your freedom and escape from the confines of the prison you've created for yourself. Escaping from this reality creates a safe place where you can be the person you always have wanted to be and were meant to be.

Aiming for perfection and pleasing everyone creates life paralysis. This means it keeps your life at a standstill. I have come to learn that by living my truth and facing my fears, I have been blessed enough to help other women do the same. Having that form of example is powerful and I often thank God for that. Don't let the fear of what other people think stop you from living the life you were born to live.

It is imperative that you recognize that people's beliefs about you do NOT define you. When you focus on pleasing others, a disconnect forms between who you truly are and the self that you present to the world. You start living your life to please others and for the accolades as a result. The problem with this is that it is exhausting because you are not being authentic. Not even Jesus could please everyone, therefore putting that unrealistic expectation on yourself is only a set up for failure.

To avoid being inauthentic, find ways to strengthen your true sense of self. People pleasing and perfectionism are like shields that hide and protect your true self. We adopt these concepts in our life to feel valuable and worthy. The more pleasing and perfecting you do, the more you become out of touch with yourself. In turn, you no longer know what you like, what you believe, what's important to you, or even who you truly are because so much of your time and effort is spent trying to be what others want you to be. This is a sad reality. I believe that we are all intentionally made unique. No one ever got anywhere by being someone else. Remember that when it feels tempting.

"Finding yourself" can feel like a big endeavor (and it may be), but you don't have to do it all at once. Bit by bit, begin to explore and experiment with things that you like...not things that others believe you should like. Self-discovery is a lifelong process because we are all constantly changing and growing. What is so exciting is that you are always expanding your potential.

You can't allow your self-worth to be dependent on other people's approval of you. If you do, I promise you will never be good enough. One of the biggest shifts that you can make is to increase your own positive self-talk. Another shift you can make is increasing your level of self-care, meaning to take good care of yourself by engaging in things that you enjoy. By beginning to give yourself more love and acceptance, you can become less dependent on other people for making you feel confident. It can be exceptionally difficult with social media all around us. Just remember what you see on the screen has nothing to do with what is going on behind the scene. You may see your old classmate taking the perfect family photo at the apple orchard, but you have no clue that she is on the brink of divorce and that her son threw chocolate all over her backseat on the way to the family fun day. One thing that I always recommend to my clients is to take a social media hiatus. That may mean you break for a month, a week or even a day. That break will give you time to focus on you and not on others. It will also help you to avoid the comparison trap. Another thing I challenge my clients to do is write down their personal goals without talking to anyone about them. If you want to quit your job and open up your own piano studio, the last thing you need is your mother telling you how much of a poor choice you will be making. Doing this activity gives you chance to get in tune with yourself and what you truly want. It also helps you not to feel like you have to be perfect. I challenge you to try to make some changes in your life today. Eckhart Tolle says "It is not uncommon for people to spend their whole life waiting to start living." Do not wait that long.

__Reflection__

Who were you before others told you who you had to be?

How often does the fear of what other people think stop you from doing something?

Who are the people in your life that you are trying to please?

What can you do to get in touch with your authentic self?

How to Get Over Being a Perfectionist

"You were born to be real not to be perfect."
-Unknown

It's great to be aware of our flaws. The trouble lies in trying to figure out how to handle them. Being a perfectionist is a hard process to overcome. I say this because even though I have strategies to work through it I often fall back into the trap, because it is a habit that takes time to break. The other reason perfection is tough to work through is because at one point or another it benefited you. For example maybe you drew the perfect family collage in high school and you're still holding on the reaction you got from the teacher. In that case using your perfectionism worked for you. On the opposite end maybe you slacked on a big work project and the consequence was not so good. Using your perfectionistic tendencies would have worked for you and now you think of why you should have used them. To some extent perfectionism works in our favor, therefore it can be challenging to overcome. I know that perfectionism seems beneficial, but I want to share that it is not. I know this from all that I lost in aiming for the perfect life. Here are some key strategies to overcome your perfectionism:

1. Brainstorm on how perfectionism has impacted you.
The first thing you need to do is to write down all of the things that perfectionism has gotten in the way of. I actually want you to write it down, because then you are forced to face it. Perfectionists often believe that they're committed to excellence, but they're actually avoiding feelings of inadequacy. If you're a perfectionist, ask yourself why. What do you think you will gain with this behavior? What does it cost you? Do you take pleasure in being perfect? How do you feel when you're less than perfect?

2. Identify all of the tasks that you have to accomplish.
Your goal is to stay focused on the most important activities. Perfectionists spend too much time on minor details therefore losing sight of the goal. Ask yourself which activities will yield the most results for the time spent. Refuse to get consumed in small tasks that take away the effort you put into the task in whole. When you focus on the big picture, all of the details cannot consume or overwhelm you.

3. Learn to accept being less than perfect.

Notice that no one else cares if something is less than perfect. The person that is making a big deal out of it is YOU! You don't need to beat everyone. I am firm believer that you just have to do your best and keep aiming to be better than you were yesterday. This is not the same thing as looking to be perfect. Instead, strive to attain a high level of quality with a reasonable amount of effort and time. When you make this shift you will notice a difference in regards to your effort. Things that did not seem perfect will now appear good enough, because you know that you did your best.

4. Include someone else.

Try to step outside of yourself. The reason this is important is because we are truly our own worst enemy. When you receive the perspective of other people it allows you to get more accurate and honest feedback. Most people will highlight how great your work is and at best they will be able to bring attention to small details that you need to change. They will likely never tell you to waste an extensive amount of time on mundane tasks where you are aiming for perfection.

5. Rid yourself of the "all or nothing" mentality.

"Things never work out in my favor" or "I am always ruining things" - does this sound familiar? My immediate family are all high achievers and therefore I never felt good enough. I constantly fell into the trap of all or nothing thinking and it never fixed anything, in fact it made it worse. In order to get out of that bad thinking pattern, you need to accept that it is o.k. to do *something* wrong and it is o.k. to do so*mething* right. When you are able to embrace that there can be a middle ground and that it is not always all or nothing, you will incorporate more compromising into your decision making. It also helps you not to feel like it has to be all one way.

6. Celebrate every part of the process.

Embrace both the victory and the failure. There will be ups in life and there will be downs. There is not one person on this earth (outside of Jesus) who got every single thing right in life. We are human after all so we are bound to fail from time to time. Those failures and setbacks have a great purpose. They serve to show us the wrong that we were doing and the changes and improvements that need to be made. Too many people run from failure or try to hide it. That behavior pattern just reinforces the failure because you never have a chance to grow from it. Learn to embrace the entire journey, and not just the good and easy part allows you to really learn and to grow.

7. **Reward yourself.**
It is hard work to face your fears and change old ways of doing things. It is hard work to go from everything having to be perfect to putting your best foot forward. It is a true mindset shift and that is a MAJOR adjustment. Give yourself grace. This process is not for the faint of heart. Be sure to take the time to reward yourself for all the hard work you are doing. Rewards don't have to monetary. They can include taking a break or spending time with an old friend, etc. Basically, allow your reward to be something that will encourage you to keep going and something that does not keep you from still being able to put your best foot forward.

If you discover that you're a perfectionist, practice each day doing something well, but not perfectly. It may take a while, but soon enough, you'll be enjoying the benefits of excellence rather than the disadvantages of perfectionism. Start small and then build up to the larger things. This will give you the skills and strategies to prepare for making progress and not solely seeking perfection.

Reflection

1. What strategies can you implement starting today to work through your perfectionism?

2. What are ways in which you can reward your efforts?

3. What can you do to avoid giving up?

It's Time to Start Over

"Strive for progress….NOT perfection, for progress will always take you farther than perfection."
- Nicolya

Changing your perfectionism perspective is not something that happens overnight. It is something that takes work, dedication and focus. It also takes practice. Realistically you did not become a perfectionist overnight. It happened over time. Be patient with yourself through this process. You will learn a lot about yourself. Learn what you can and continue to grow. If you fall off one day, that's okay, pick back up the next. Whatever you do, don't stop. Keep implementing the strategies in this book. In time you will see a MAJOR shift in the way you respond to the things you do.

Now that you are aware of your perfectionism and how to work through it, you must move forward. Chose to forgive yourself. Forgive yourself for putting unreasonable expectations on yourself. The truth is that we all have character flaws. You are just awesome enough to recognize that you are limited in your human state and now you can grow. Here is a saying that I was given a year ago. I read this when I want to initiate a fresh start. Please feel free to use this as well:

I start fresh.
Each day is an opportunity to start anew. I make a fresh beginning. I experiment more. Just doing one thing differently creates a chain reaction. I find myself branching out and enjoying exciting adventures. My confidence increases and my life seems fuller.
I stop and think before I act. I make conscious choices instead of operating on autopilot. I watch out for self-limiting beliefs and habits that make me less effective. I develop new routines that leverage my strengths and prepare me for success.
I forgive myself and others. I let go of resentment and disappointments.
I replenish my energy levels. I give my body adequate rest and sleep. I eat nourishing whole foods and exercise daily. I find relaxation methods that work for me.
I evaluate my goals. I drop low-priority projects so that I can devote more time to the activities that give me the greatest sense of meaning and accomplishment.
I follow through. I give my ideas a chance to come to fruition. I do my research, gather the necessary resources, and write out specific action plans. I give myself deadlines and assess my progress.

I embrace change. I reframe losses as opportunities. I find a balance between stagnation and chaos. I give myself credit for being resilient and adaptable. I become more proactive.

Today, I reboot my life. I leave the past behind and take a giant step forward. I focus on being happy and productive.

After finishing this book, I hope you are aware that you are not alone in your struggles. I wrote this book after speaking to hundreds of women that gave up on their goals all because they could not achieve them perfectly. I wanted an opportunity to share with these women that I too struggled with that, but when I broke free, the floodgates opened up and allowed me the chance to start living the life that I had only dreamed about. No, I am not permanently cured of my perfectionism and I often do fall back into my old ways of thinking, but now I have strategies that I can use when I am battling with myself.

When I sat down to write this book, I had no idea that it would be the hardest book for me to write. Although this is the sixth book I have authored (Eighth if you include the two collaborative books I have done) I wanted it to be perfect. Since I wanted it to be perfect I constantly procrastinated, because it seemed like nothing I was doing was ever going to be good enough. Then I remembered that I was blocking the chance for me to bless other women with this information. I immediately knew I needed to implement the steps to push me past the fantasy that I had to be perfect. I do not believe it was at all a coincidence that I was tested while writing this book. In fact I am convinced that it was intentional. It happened the way it did so that you as my reader would know that you are not alone. So that you would know that I too struggle from time to time, but I am able to pick myself up and still reach my goals. This is very possible for you and I am excited to see what you will accomplish now that you have the skills to make it happen.

While perfectionism and procrastination may have plagued you in the past, you now have the tools to create a new future — not tomorrow, but *today*. Do not get discouraged. Remember, breaking the cycle is a process. It will take time to break years of old habits. Do not beat yourself up if and when you fall back into procrastination mode. Recognize that you are doing it and commit to trying one or more of the tips suggested in this book. Your efforts will take you much farther than striving for things that are nonexistent.

Reflection

1. What are your biggest takeaways from this book?

2. What changes will you make from here forward to work through your perfectionist tendencies?

3. How do you think these changes will positively impact your life?

4. What have you learned from being a perfectionist?

Find Your Balance in Imperfection

"Perfectionism rarely begets perfection, or satisfaction - only
disappointment."
-Ryan Holiday

Paul Arden says "Too many people spend too much time trying to perfect something before they actually do it. Instead of waiting for perfection, run with what you've got, and fix it along the way..." This is the quote that I have lived by. The key to success is to start before everything is perfect! Choose success when you have no time, choose success when you just failed, choose success even when it's hard, choose success when you are sad, choose success every time and success will then choose you! Don't wait for perfection to start to live!

Too many dreams have been shattered or pushed aside for my fear of not being perfect. Now when I have goals, whether or not I believe they will go perfectly I jump and build my wings on the way down. Yes I have fallen, but more importantly I have succeeded. I have gained the opportunity to grow more in touch with my authentic self and I love it.

No one in this fallen world is perfect. Not your friend from high school who posts her perfect life on Facebook, not your ex-boyfriend that seems happy, not your pastor, not your grandma...nobody! It does not matter how flawless their life seems, how happy their life appears, it does not even matter what lies they are telling you. We are all human and by that word alone it is impossible to be perfect. As humans, all we can do is strive to do our best and applaud ourselves for the attempt. Yes you may fail, but guess what? You will learn. Yes, you may struggle, but guess what? You will grow. That is life.

Striving to be perfect is the best recipe for failure since it is impossible to attain. We all make mistakes. The key is to recognize the mistakes you have made and then learn from them for the next time. Do not engage yourself in self-abuse by saying hateful or hurtful things to yourself or even about yourself. That will never solve the problem either. Do not overwhelm yourself with guilt. Focus on doing your best. If you set a goal work toward it. If you don't feel good enough try it anyways. If you made a mistake learn from it. That, my friend, is progress and progress will ALWAYS be better than perfection.

Appendix A: Perfectionism Journal

Use this journal once a week for the next 4 weeks to work through your perfectionistic tendencies and learn to replace them with healthy habits. This journal will help bring awareness to the habits that have influenced your thoughts of having to be a perfectionist.

Week: _____

Today I showed perfectionism by:

What outcome did this cause?

What could I have done instead?

What did I learn from this?

What is one strategy that I will implement starting now to work through my perfectionism?

Who can help support me on this journey?

Do I believe that I have made progress?

How did my attempts to change my perfectionistic patterns work?

Week: _____

Today I showed perfectionism by:

What outcome did this cause?

What could I have done instead?

What did I learn from this?

What is one strategy that I will implement starting now to work through my perfectionism?

Who can help support me on this journey?

Do I believe that I have made progress?

How did my attempts to change my perfectionistic patterns work?

Week: _____

Today I showed perfectionism by:

What outcome did this cause?

What could I have done instead?

What did I learn from this?

What is one strategy that I will implement starting now to work through my perfectionism?

Who can help support me on this journey?

Do I believe that I have made progress?

How did my attempts to change my perfectionistic patterns work?

Week: _____

Today I showed perfectionism by:

What outcome did this cause?

What could I have done instead?

What did I learn from this?

What is one strategy that I will implement starting now to work through my perfectionism?

Who can help support me on this journey?

Do I believe that I have made progress?

How did my attempts to change my perfectionistic patterns work?

Note to my readers

I accept less than perfection.

Perfection is the very enemy of my happiness, productivity, and my mental health. I am willing to challenge my expectations to enhance my life.

My ability to accept less than perfection allows happiness to enter and stay in my life. Perfection is therefore an obstacle to happiness which I am not willing to allow. From here forward, I will do my best and accept the results. I will strive for excellence and avoid seeking perfection. By avoiding the need for perfection, I will be more peaceful and happier. The people in my life will also be happy.

I get much more accomplished when I am free of the need to be perfect. The need to be perfect can trigger procrastination. Now that I will be free from perfection it will be easier for me to get started on my work each day. I will use my time wisely and accept whatever life brings. My best is good enough. Having this attitude increases my productivity.

I am more content and relaxed when I remember that perfection is a myth. Accepting the results of my efforts ensures that

I sleep better and enjoy my spare time more. The desire for perfection creates stress and anxiety.

I realize that perfection is an impossibility for others, too. I maintain reasonable standards for the people in my life, but I avoid having unreasonable expectations. I accept others as they are because I love them.

Today, I am doing my best and accepting the outcomes I produce. I am content when I allow others and myself to be less than perfect.

You are perfect with every imperfection!

About Nicolya

Nicolya Williams is the type of woman who pursues her goals with passion and determination. She is dedicated to helping other women conquer their chaos and reach their goals. Nicolya is a personal development coach, radio host, best-selling author, and blogger for women. Nicolya graduated from The Ohio State University (B.A., Psychology) and obtained her M.Ed. from the University of Dayton with a focus on Clinical Counseling and School Counseling. Nicolya is currently a doctoral student with a focus on Transformational Leadership. Nicolya holds a Coach Practitioner certificate and is licensed as both a Community Counselor and School Counselor, with a Chemical Dependency Counselor Assistant license.
Nicolya, a lifelong learner, strives to continue her personal growth through reading and interacting with her social and spiritual community. She is an avid reader and is devoted to building up her own strong women: her daughters, Kaelyn and Kamryn. Nicolya is committed to creating a space for women to be heard and successful! You can connect with Nicolya at www.nicolyawilliams.com or on all social media platforms via @NicolyaWilliams.

Clarity Cove Publishing
~We publish books that the world needs~
Clarity Cove Publishing was created by Nicolya Williams. Clarity Cove Publishing connects with powerful, determined and driven women to help them turn their message into their masterpiece. We offer publishing services, writing assistance, marketing strategies and much more. Our vision is to foster creativity, encourage risk taking and increase clarity around your book writing goals. Our authors have an opportunity to get their message out into the masses without losing their authenticity in the process.
To inquire about publishing with us or getting support along your publishing journey reach out to us at
http://www.nicolyawilliams.com/clarity-cove-publishing/
or email at claritycove@nicolyawilliams.com